MW00472296

Wherever You Go, You're Always My Friend

Original Verse and Illustrations by

Heidi Satterberg

HARVEST HOUSE PUBLISHERS
Eugene, Oregon 97402

Wherever You Go, You're Always My Friend

Text Copyright © 2001 by Harvest House Publishers
Eugene, Oregon 97402

ISBN 0-7369-0598-7

Artwork designs and original verse are reproduced under license from
© Arts Uniq' ®, Inc., Cookeville, TN and may not be reproduced without
permission. For more information regarding art prints featured in this book,
please contact:

> Arts Uniq'
> P.O. Box 3085
> Cookeville, TN 38502
> 1.800.223.5020

Design and production by Garborg Design Works, Minneapolis, Minnesota

Scripture quotations are taken from the Holy Bible, New International
Version®, Copyright © 1973, 1978, 1984 by the International Bible Society.
Used by permission of Zondervan Publishing House.

Harvest House Publishers has made every effort to trace the ownership of
all poems and quotes. In the event of a question arising from the use of a
poem or quote, we regret any error made and will be pleased to make the
necessary correction in future editions of this book.

All rights reserved. No part of this publication may be reproduced, stored
in a retrieval system, or transmitted in any form or by any means—electronic,
mechanical, digital, photocopy, recording, or any other—except for brief
quotations in printed reviews, without the prior permission of the publisher.

Printed in China.

01 02 03 04 05 06 07 08 09 10 /IM / 10 9 8 7 6 5 4 3 2 1

Our friendship knows no boundaries,
Even when we're apart.
From east to west, north to south,
We're connected heart-to-heart.

May the road rise to meet you,
May the wind be always at your back,
May the sun shine warmly on your face,
The rains fall soft upon your fields.
And until we meet again,
May God hold you in the palm of His hand.

IRISH BLESSING

You're willing to let me lean on you

When alone I cannot stand.

You know just when to speak, or not,

Or to lend a helping hand.

Friends are born,
not made.

HENRY ADAMS

4

Italy

The better you know someone, the less there is to say. Or, maybe there's less that needs to be said.

AUTHOR UNKNOWN

A real friend is one who walks in when the rest of the world walks out.

WALTER WINCHELL

There comes that mysterious meeting in life when someone acknowledges who we are and what we can be, igniting the circuits of our highest potential.

RUSTY BERKUS

In a friend you find a second self.

ISABELLE NORTON

7

親友

Heidi Joy

Heidi Satterberg ©

Japan

It didn't take long for us to know
That our friendship
would continue to blossom.
Just like a rare and fragrant flower,
I find it totally awesome.

A friend is someone
who reaches out for
your hand...and
touches your heart.

KATHLEEN GROVE

9

$\mathcal{B}$ecause of the trust I have in you,
My secrets I freely share.
I build no walls around my heart,
For I know you truly care.

$\mathcal{W}$alking with a friend in
the dark is better than
walking alone in the light.

HELEN KELLER

China

Don't be dismayed
at good-byes.
A farewell is
necessary before
you can
meet again.
And meeting
again, after
moments or
lifetimes, is
certain for those
who are friends.

RICHARD BACH

Those who loved you and were
helped by you will remember
you when forget-me-nots have
withered. Carve your name on
hearts, not on marble.

CHARLES H. SPURGEON

A friend is someone who
understands your past, believes
in your future, and accepts you
today just the way you are.

ROBERT LOUIS STEVENSON

Heidi Joy

Heidi Satterberg ©

Germany

14

$\mathcal{M}$any friends may come our way;

Though some won't last life-long.

Yet our friendship has stayed secure...

Like a fortress, true and strong.

Go often to the house of thy friend,

for weeds choke the unused path.

RALPH WALDO EMERSON

Your friendship means so much to me;
You're special and unique.
Incredible qualities you possess,
They make you "magnifique."

Friends are the chocolate
chips in the cookie of life.

AUTHOR UNKNOWN

Heidi Joy

Heidi Satterberg ©

France

The only way to have
a friend is to be one.

RALPH WALDO EMERSON

What is a friend? I will tell

you . . . it is someone with

whom you dare to be yourself.

FRANK CRANE

Wherever
you are, it is
your friends
who make
your world.

WILLIAM JAMES

19

Heidi Joy

Heidi Satterberg ©

Netherlands

$\mathcal{J}$ust you "being you"
Brings such color to my world.
Your life is like a rainbow ribbon
Which dazzles when unfurled.

Friends are those
rare people who

ask how you are
and then wait to

hear the answer.

AUTHOR UNKNOWN

Whenever I'm feeling discouraged,

You always seem to know.

You're free with words of encouragement,

I bask in the warmth of their glow.

Friends are the
sunshine of life.

JOHN HAY

Heidi Joy

Hawaii

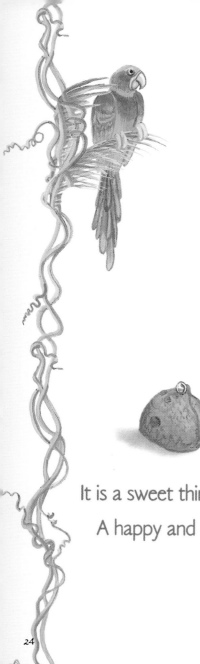

Let us be grateful
to people who make
us happy; they
are the charming
gardeners who make
our souls blossom.

MARCEL PROUST

It is a sweet thing, friendship, a dear balm,
A happy and auspicious bird of calm...

SHELLEY

There are moments in life
when the voice of a friend
can sound like a choir
of angels to the heart.

AUTHOR UNKNOWN

Heidi Joy

Heidi Satterberg ©

Yellowstone

$\mathcal{S}$ometimes when life's pressures build,

I'm as grouchy as a bear.

But as a "faithful," loving friend,

You let me know you care.

If I had a single
flower for every
time I think of you,
I could walk forever
in my garden.

CLAUDIA GRANDI

27

When I'm feeling "down and under,"
Or just a little blue,
You seem to know just what I need
When I don't have a clue.

Thus nature has no love for solitude,
and always leans, as it were, on some
support; and the sweetest support is
found in the most intimate friendship.

CICERO

Heidi Joy

Heidi Satterberg ©

Australia

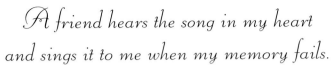

*A friend hears the song in my heart
and sings it to me when my memory fails.*

AUTHOR UNKNOWN

My friends are my estate. Forgive me then the avarice to hoard them. They tell me those who were poor early have different views of gold. I don't know how that is. God is not so wary as we, else He would give us no friends, lest we forget Him.

EMILY DICKINSON

I'd like to be the sort of friend
That you have been to me.
I'd like to be the help that you've been
Always glad to be;
I'd like to mean as much to you
Each minute of the day,
As you have meant, old friend of mine,
To me along the way.

EDGAR GUEST

Friendship is a single soul dwelling in two bodies.

ARISTOTLE

31

Heidi Joy

Heidi Satterberg ©

Africa

$\mathcal{I}$'ve searched the whole world over,
And I'm not surprised to find...
That you're the greatest friend on earth.
You're truly one-of-a-kind.

$\mathcal{N}$ever shall $\mathcal{I}$ forget the days $\mathcal{I}$ spend
with you. $\mathcal{C}$ontinue to be my friend, as
you will always find me yours.

LUDWIG VAN BEETHOVEN

33

I'm grateful for our history;
Our friendship's been sublime.
We built it well, step-by-step,
To stand the test of time.

A friend loves at all times.

THE BOOK OF PROVERBS

Heidi Joy

Heidi Soderberg ©

Egypt

For when two beings who are not friends are near each other there is no meeting, and when friends are far apart there is no separation.

SIMONE WEIL

*A friend is a gift
you give yourself.*

ROBERT LOUIS STEVENSON

I don't remember how we
    happened to meet each other.
I don't remember who got along
    with whom first.
All I can remember is all of us
    together...always.

AUTHOR UNKNOWN

Heidi Joy

Heidi Satterberg ©

Norway

It makes me want to celebrate
To have a friend like you.
You are God's special gift to me;
You're valued through and through.

And Pooh said to Piglet,
"Life is so much
friendlier with two."

A. A. MILNE

$\mathcal{S}$ometimes I tend to guard my heart
When I feel like life's a trial.
You show me that God cares for me,
Which always makes me smile!

We're not sisters by birth, but we
knew from the start,
Something put us together to be
sisters of the heart.

AUTHOR UNKNOWN

Heidi Joy

Heidi Salterberg ©

England

But friendship is precious,

not only in the shade, but

in the sunshine of life; and

thanks to a benevolent

arrangement of things,

the greater part of life is sunshine.

THOMAS JEFFERSON

Think where man's glory most

begins and ends,

And say my glory was I had

such friends.

WILLIAM YEATS

42

If I had one gift that
I could give you,
my friend, it would
be the ability to
see yourself as
others see you,
because only then
would you know
how extremely
special you are.

B. A. BILLINGSLY

Heidi Joy

Heidi Satterberg ©

South Pole

$\mathcal{I}$'d travel to the ends-of-the-earth
For a friend as dear as you.
Over hill or dale or snow-packed trail,
Our friendship is true-blue.

$\mathcal{F}$riendship is the only cement that

will ever hold the world together.

WOODROW WILSON

*Y*our role in life lets you wear
A variety of hats.
The "amigo" one you wear so well
Is a grand one! My congrats!

*Friends warm you with their presence,
Trust you with their secrets,
And remember you in their prayers.*

AUTHOR UNKNOWN

Mexico

We are all travelers in the wilderness of
this world, and the best we can find in
our travels is an honest friend.

ROBERT LOUIS STEVENSON

Once in a while you meet someone and soon
you discover the two of you are truly something special to each other...you
share your thoughts and feelings
so relaxed, so openly, and
right away you know your
friendship's meant to be.

GARY HARRINGTON

If, out of time, I could pick one moment
And keep it shining, always new,
Of all the days that I have lived,
I'd pick the moment I met you.

AUTHOR UNKNOWN